I0478181

So You're Sorta Thinking
About Starting an
awesomely effective

Content
Marketing
Strategy?

⌐A Beginner's Guide to Content Marketing for
Small Business Owners: Simple Steps to Grow
Your Brand and Engage Your Audience⌐

frank
dappah

So You're Sorta Thinking About Starting an awesomely effective

Content
Marketing
Strategy?

A Beginner's Guide to Content Marketing for Small Business Owners: Simple Steps to Grow Your Brand and Engage Your Audience

frank
dappah

OSTRICH®

Publisher's Disclaimer:

The information contained in this publication is for general informational purposes only. While we have made every effort to provide accurate and up-to-date information, we make no representations or warranties of any kind, express or implied, about the completeness, accuracy, reliability, suitability, or availability with respect to the content contained herein. Any reliance you place on such information is therefore strictly at your own risk.

Content Accuracy:

The content in this publication is based on the knowledge and information available at the time of writing. However, developments in the field may occur after publication, and the publisher cannot guarantee that the information provided will always be complete, accurate, or up-to-date. Readers are advised to consult additional sources and seek professional advice where necessary.

Editorial Responsibility:

The views and opinions expressed by the authors, contributors, and editors of this publication are their own and do not necessarily reflect the views of Ostrich Publishers. The publisher disclaims any liability or responsibility for any errors, omissions, or inaccuracies that may be present in the content.

Legal Compliance:

While every effort has been made to ensure compliance with all applicable laws and regulations, the publisher cannot be held responsible for any legal implications or consequences arising from the use or misuse of the information in this publication. Readers are advised to familiarize themselves with the relevant laws and seek legal counsel if necessary.

Third-Party Content:

This publication may include content from third-party sources, including but not limited to quotes, references, or excerpts. Ostrich Publishers does not endorse or guarantee the accuracy, reliability, or suitability of any third-party content referenced in this publication. Any reliance on such content is at the reader's own discretion and risk.

External Links:

This publication may contain links to external websites or resources. Ostrich Publishers has no control over the nature, content, and availability of those sites or resources. The inclusion of any links does not necessarily imply a recommendation or endorsement by the publisher. Ostrich Publishers shall not be held liable for any damages or losses arising from the use of such external links.

Copyright:

All rights reserved. No part of this publication may be reproduced, distributed, or transmitted in any form or by any means, including photocopying, recording, or other electronic or mechanical methods, without the prior written permission of the publisher, except in the case of brief quotations embodied in critical reviews and certain other noncommercial uses permitted by copyright law.

Contact Information:

For inquiries regarding this publication, please contact:

Ostrich Publishers
Charlotte, NC
U.S.A
Email: admin@ostrichpress.com
Website: www.ostrichpress.com

Disclaimer Updates:

Ostrich Publishers reserves the right to amend or update this disclaimer at any time without prior notice. It is the responsibility of the readers to regularly review this disclaimer for any changes.

Last Updated:
May 2024

DEDICATION

To my incredible wife and business partner, Bernice,

Thank you for twelve years of unwavering support, endless patience, and for being the glue that holds both our business and my newfound running habits together. You've not only stood by me through countless business meetings and brainstorming sessions but also through every late-night run, every blistered foot, and every moment when I desperately needed to hear, "Call, don't text."

Your dedication to our partnership is matched only by your ability to remind me to call you when I need help— even though answering calls while juggling spreadsheets is no easy feat. I admire your bravery in navigating the chaotic world of emails and phone calls, especially when I'm out on the trails, miles away and relying on your prompt responses... or at least your enthusiastic attempts to respond.

You're always just a phone call away during my long runs, even if your phone skills sometimes leave me laughing harder than my worst running mishaps. Whether it's deciphering your "quick call" before I hit the pavement or trying to interpret your texts when I know a good ol' phone call is what's needed, your unique approach keeps things interesting and keeps me safe.

Thank you for being my emergency contact, my cheerleader, and the reason I have a solid excuse to stop and stretch every now and then. Your mantra, "Call, don't text," has become the lifeline I need when the miles get tough and the pavement seems endless. And let's be honest, without your ability to not always be glued to your phone, my runs would lack that essential touch of unpredictability—and possibly more humor than necessary.

Here's to many more years of partnership, laughter, and miles run side by side (even if mine are mostly solo). You're my favorite running buddy, even if it's only through the phone.

With all my love and gratitude,

Frank

So You're Sorta Thinking
About Starting an
awesomely effective

Content
Marketing
Strategy?

A Beginner's Guide to Content Marketing for
Small Business Owners: Simple Steps to Grow
Your Brand and Engage Your Audience

frank
dappah

TABLE OF CONTENTS

CONTENT MARKETING STRATEGY

PREFACE

When I first started exploring content marketing as part of my overall sales and marketing responsibilities at Salesfully.com, it felt overwhelming—especially as a small business owner. Between juggling day-to-day tasks and figuring out how to connect with our audience of mostly small sales teams, the idea of creating a well-rounded content marketing strategy seemed like just another daunting item on my endless to-do list. And I know I'm not alone in feeling this way. Many small business owners, just like you, are trying to navigate the complexities of content marketing while keeping their businesses running smoothly.

This book, **"So You're Kinda Thinking About, Looking Into Executing a Content Marketing Strategy?"**, is my attempt to make this process a bit more approachable. I wanted to create something that feels like having a real conversation—no fancy jargon, no intimidating frameworks, just practical advice for folks who are starting out, trying to get their footing. It's a journey I've been on myself, and I know it's worth it. Content marketing has the potential to transform your business, build lasting relationships with your audience, and help you stand out in a crowded marketplace.

We're going to explore everything from understanding what content marketing actually means, to figuring out what types of content best suit your brand, to using AI and emerging trends to your advantage. My goal is to guide you through this process step by step, giving you the confidence to dive in and start creating content that genuinely resonates with your audience.

Whether you're a solopreneur just getting started or a small business owner with a growing team, this book is here to help you think about content marketing in a way that makes sense for your unique needs. Let's take this journey together, one step at a time. I promise that by the end, you'll feel equipped not just to execute a content marketing strategy, but to do it in a way that feels authentic and achievable.

— Frank Dappah, Founder and CEO of Salesfully.com

CHAPTER # 1: CONTENT MARKETING BASICS

Content marketing. It's one of those terms that gets thrown around a lot, and if you're just getting started, it can feel like everyone's already an expert except you. But here's the thing: content marketing is actually a lot more straightforward than it seems, and if you're a small business owner, it can be one of the most powerful tools you have at your disposal. So let's break it down—what is content marketing, why does it work, and how can you start using it to help your business thrive?

What Is Content Marketing?

At its core, content marketing is about creating and sharing valuable content to attract and engage your target audience. It's not about pushing a product or making a hard sell—it's about building trust and providing something genuinely useful. Whether it's a blog post that explains a concept your audience cares about, a video that solves a problem, or a social media post that entertains, content marketing is about meeting people where they are and giving them something they find valuable.

Let's make this more tangible. Imagine you're running a small local coffee shop. Sure, you can put out ads about your latest promotions or new menu items, but what if instead, you wrote a blog post about **"The Best Ways to Brew Coffee at Home"?** Or what if you posted a video on Instagram showing your baristas sharing their favorite coffee-making tips? Suddenly, you're not just selling coffee—you're creating a connection. You're giving people something they can use, something they can share, and something that makes them think of your shop when they're ready for their next cup of joe.

Why Does Content Marketing Work?

Content marketing works because it's built on the foundation of trust and relationships. Unlike traditional advertising, which interrupts people and asks for their attention, content marketing invites people in. It gives them something they want or need—whether that's information, inspiration, or entertainment—and, in return, builds a relationship that's based on value, not just a sales pitch.

People buy from businesses they trust. And trust is built by showing up consistently, offering value, and demonstrating that you understand your audience's needs. Content marketing allows you to do just that. When you consistently put out content that resonates with your audience, they begin to see you as a trusted source. They come back to you for more information, and when the time comes that they need a product or service you offer, guess who's already top of mind? You.

Another key reason content marketing works is that it's incredibly versatile. Whether you're writing articles, making videos, creating infographics, or even sending out email newsletters, content marketing lets you adapt your message to suit your audience. You can share your story in a way that's authentic and unique to you, without being confined by the limits of traditional advertising.

How Content Marketing Helps Small Businesses

Now, let's talk about why content marketing is especially powerful for small businesses. You might be thinking, **"I don't have the kind of budget that big brands have for marketing,"** and that's exactly why content marketing is your secret weapon. With content marketing, you're not competing on who has the most money—you're competing on who can provide the most value.

Let's go back to our coffee shop example. You're not Starbucks, and you don't have their advertising budget. But what you do have is a story. You have your passion for great coffee, your loyal customers, and your deep knowledge of your craft. Through content marketing, you can share all of that with your audience. You can connect with your community in a way that feels genuine, and that's something even the biggest brands can't always do.

Content marketing also helps you stand out from the crowd. When you create content that's unique to your brand—whether it's your take on a popular topic or something deeply personal—you're giving people a reason to choose you over the competition. You're not just another coffee shop, another gym, or another boutique. You're a brand with a voice, with something to say, and that makes all the difference.

Getting Started with Content Marketing

So, how do you get started with content marketing? First things first: you need to know your audience. Who are they? What do they care about? What kinds of problems are they trying to solve, and how can you help them? The better you understand your audience, the easier it will be to create content that resonates with them.

Start by thinking about the questions your customers ask you most often. If you're a florist, maybe people often ask you how to keep their flowers fresh longer. That's a perfect topic for a blog post or a short video. If you're a personal trainer, maybe people always want to know the best exercises for beginners—that's great content for a social media post or an email newsletter.

Once you know your audience and their pain points, the next step is to choose your content types. You don't need to be everywhere or do everything. Start with one or two types of content that feel achievable and sustainable. Maybe you like writing—great, start with blog posts. Maybe you're more comfortable talking than writing—perfect, start with videos. The key is to choose something that feels natural to you so that you can stay consistent.

Consistency Is Key

If there's one thing I want you to take away from this chapter, it's this: consistency is everything. Content marketing isn't about creating one amazing piece of content and then calling it a day. It's about showing up, week after week, building momentum, and creating something that lasts.

You don't need to put out a new blog post every day, or even every week. But whatever schedule you choose, stick with it. Maybe it's one blog post a month, or one video every two weeks— whatever it is, stay consistent. Your audience needs to know they can rely on you, and consistency builds trust.

Content Marketing Is a Long Game

One final thing to remember: content marketing is a long game. It's not about getting immediate results—it's about building something that grows over time. You might not see a flood of new customers after your first blog post, and that's okay. Content marketing takes time to gain traction, but when it does, the benefits are lasting.

Think of it like planting seeds. You're not going to see a tree overnight, but if you keep watering those seeds, eventually you'll have something strong and sustainable. The same goes for your content. Keep creating, keep sharing, keep connecting, and over time, you'll see the results.

CHAPTER # 2: GETTING STARTED WITH AI IN CONTENT MARKETING

If you're a business owner or planning to become one, chances are you've already considered how to market your brand in the smartest way possible—especially when you're working on a tight budget. Content marketing, as you may already know, is one of the most cost-effective and impactful tools out there. But what if I told you that using AI in content marketing could make your strategies even more effective, efficient, and scalable? Let's dive into how AI is changing the content marketing landscape for small businesses and solopreneurs like you.

As someone who oversees content generation for my company, I've found AI tools to be a real game-changer when it comes to managing content creation more effectively. Content marketing is already a broad, time-consuming endeavor, but AI has helped us streamline our process, allowing us to focus more on the creative aspects of our strategy. From brainstorming blog topics to optimizing SEO and even helping with writing drafts, AI tools have allowed us to get more done with fewer resources. So let's break down how AI can help you do the same.

Speed Up Content Creation

One of the biggest challenges in content marketing is creating high-quality content consistently. You need blog posts, articles, social media updates, email campaigns—and each of these requires a lot of time to craft. AI tools like ChatGPT, Jasper, and Writesonic can help you draft content more quickly by providing ideas, outlines, and even full paragraphs that are relevant to your topic. This means you can spend less time staring at a blank screen and more time refining your message to best fit your audience.

These tools are especially useful when you're feeling stuck or just can't seem to get started. Need a headline? AI can generate ten in seconds. Trying to think of a catchy intro for your blog? AI's got you covered. A recent report by Forrester found that businesses using AI in their content creation processes saw a 20-30% increase in productivity. This means more content in less time—and with a small team, that's a major advantage.

Personalize Content for Your Audience

You already know that understanding your audience is the cornerstone of content marketing. AI takes that understanding to a whole new level by allowing you to personalize your content in ways that wouldn't be possible manually. Tools like HubSpot's AI features and Persado use machine learning to analyze audience data and create messages that resonate on a deeper level. They can even adjust the tone and style based on what performs best with different segments of your audience.

Imagine being able to serve specific articles or offers to users based on their previous behavior on your site. AI can help you do exactly that, ensuring that every piece of content you produce feels more personal, and thus more valuable, to your readers. According to McKinsey, personalization can increase marketing efficiency by up to 30%, which is huge for a small business on a budget.

Optimize SEO and Content Performance

AI is also fantastic when it comes to SEO. Tools like SurferSEO, Clearscope, and SEMrush use AI to analyze top-ranking pages and identify the keywords, phrases, and structures that will help your content rank higher in search results. This means you can create SEO-optimized content without having to be an SEO expert yourself.

We've used these tools extensively, and they have made a world of difference in our visibility. SEO is one of those things that can easily feel overwhelming if you're not familiar with it, but AI simplifies the process. The right keywords, the ideal length, the correct structure—it all becomes more manageable with the right tools. According to Moz, businesses that incorporate SEO optimization tools in their content marketing strategy see, on average, a 45% increase in organic search traffic.

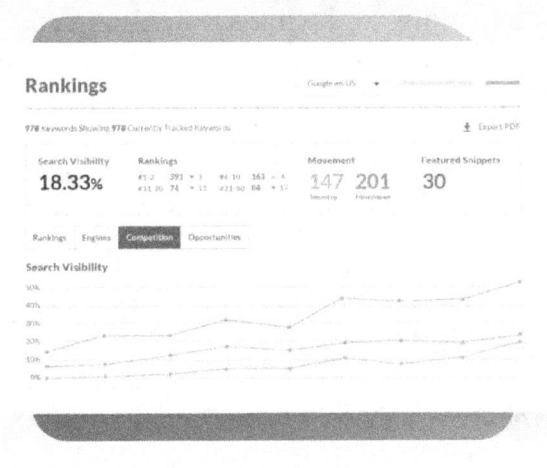

Automate Repetitive Tasks

Another great advantage of AI in content marketing is automating repetitive tasks. Whether it's scheduling posts, sending out email campaigns, or managing responses on social media, tools like Buffer, Hootsuite, and Mailchimp are incorporating AI features that can help manage these tasks more efficiently. The less time you spend on repetitive tasks, the more time you have to focus on strategy and creativity.

These tools also help you analyze performance—AI algorithms can identify what's working and what's not, giving you actionable insights to optimize your content strategy. AI analytics tools like Google Analytics 4 and HubSpot's Marketing Hub provide real-time data that helps you tweak your campaigns as they run. According to Statista, marketers who use automation tools see a 12% reduction in time spent on administrative tasks, freeing up time for more strategic work.

Understand Your Own Capabilities

It's easy to get caught up in all the different ways AI can be used in content marketing. But as with any tool, it's important to assess your resources and capabilities honestly. AI can help streamline a lot of the process, but it still requires human oversight. It's not a "set it and forget it" kind of thing. You have to be involved to make sure the content produced aligns with your brand's voice and goals.

If you're a solopreneur or part of a small team, it's crucial not to overextend yourself. AI can help you do more, but consistency is still key. You don't need to use every tool or try every tactic. Start small—maybe use an AI tool to help with SEO or to draft blog outlines—and build from there. The last thing you want is to create an overcomplicated strategy that becomes impossible to maintain. Remember, consistency builds trust, and trust is what turns a casual reader into a loyal customer.

The use of AI in content marketing has revolutionized the way small businesses can approach their marketing strategies. By speeding up content creation, personalizing messaging, optimizing for SEO, and automating repetitive tasks, AI has made content marketing more accessible and effective. However, it's also important to understand your own capabilities and to not overextend yourself. Start small, use AI as an assistant rather than a replacement, and build from there.

AI is a powerful tool that, when used wisely, can help you create the right content for the right audience at the right time. The key to success lies in balancing automation with your own creativity and understanding of your audience.

CHAPTER # 3: CONTENT TYPES AND KNOWING YOUR AUDIENCE

Now that you've got a handle on what content marketing is and how AI can help you work smarter, it's time to talk about the different types of content you can create and, more importantly, who you're creating it for. One of the biggest mistakes small business owners make when they're getting into content marketing is trying to do too much.

There's an endless number of content types— blogs, videos, social media posts, podcasts, infographics—and it's easy to feel like you need to do it all. But the truth is, you don't. What you need is the "right" content for the "right" audience.

In this chapter, we're going to break down different types of content, figure out which ones make the most sense for your audience, and explore some real-life examples of companies that have found success using each type. By the end of this chapter, you'll have a clear idea of what kind of content to focus on and how to make it count.

Know Your Audience

The first step in deciding what kind of content to create is knowing who you're talking to. I can't stress this enough: "know your audience". You can create the most amazing, beautifully produced video, but if it doesn't resonate with the people you're trying to reach, it's not going to do you much good.

So, who is your audience? Are they young professionals? Busy parents? Are they other small business owners? The better you understand them, the better you can tailor your content to their needs. Think about their problems, their desires, and how your business fits into their lives. Ask yourself questions like:

- What kind of content do they consume?
- What are their biggest challenges?
- What questions do they have that your content could answer?

Once you know who you're talking to, you can choose the content types that are most likely to reach and resonate with them.

Different Types of Content

Let's explore some of the different types of content you can use in your marketing strategy. I'm going to walk you through the most common ones, along with examples of real-life companies that have found success with each type.

1. Blog Posts

Blogging is one of the most popular and accessible types of content marketing. A well-written blog post can provide valuable information to your audience, drive traffic to your website, and help you rank higher on search engines.

Take, for example, HubSpot. HubSpot's blog is filled with articles about marketing, sales, and customer service. They've established themselves as a go-to resource for anyone looking to learn about these topics. If you're a small business owner, starting a blog can be a great way to share your expertise and attract an audience that's interested in what you do.

Pro Tip: Make sure your blog posts are optimized for search engines (SEO) by including keywords that your audience is likely to search for. Tools like Yoast can help you do this easily.

2. Videos

Video content is incredibly engaging, and it's become one of the most popular ways for people to consume information. Whether you're doing a quick explainer video, a product demo, or just sharing behind-the-scenes footage, video helps bring your brand to life.

Consider Dollar Shave Club. Their funny and straightforward launch video went viral and put them on the map. It showed personality, explained what they offered, and resonated with their target audience—men looking for an affordable, no-fuss shaving solution.

Pro Tip: You don't need fancy equipment to get started with video. A smartphone and some good lighting can do wonders. Just be authentic—people respond to real, relatable content.

3. Social Media Posts

Social media is a fantastic way to connect with your audience in real time. Whether you're posting on Instagram, Facebook, LinkedIn, or TikTok, social media allows you to share updates, engage with followers, and build a community around your brand.

Glossier, the beauty brand, is a great example of effective social media marketing. They use Instagram to showcase their products, share user-generated content, and engage directly with their followers. Their social media presence feels personal and community-driven, which has helped them build a loyal fanbase.

Pro Tip: Social media is about building relationships, not just pushing products. Share behind-the-scenes content, ask your followers questions, and interact with their comments to create a genuine connection.

4. Infographics

If you have data or information that might be hard to digest in text form, consider creating an infographic. Infographics are visually appealing and can help break down complex information in a way that's easy to understand and share.

Buffer, a social media management platform, has used infographics to share social media statistics, marketing tips, and more. These infographics are easy to share, which has helped Buffer reach a wider audience and establish themselves as experts in their field.

Pro Tip: Tools like Canva make it easy to create infographics, even if you don't have design experience. Just make sure the information you're presenting is clear and valuable to your audience.

5. Podcasts

Podcasts are another great way to reach your audience, especially if they're the type of people who like to listen on the go. Podcasts allow you to dive deep into topics, interview interesting guests, and build a connection with your listeners over time.

Patagonia, the outdoor clothing brand, has a podcast called The Patagonia Stories, where they share stories about environmental activism, outdoor adventures, and the people who inspire their brand. It aligns perfectly with their values and helps them connect with an audience that shares those same passions.

Pro Tip: You don't need to create a long, highly produced podcast to be successful. Short, focused episodes that provide value to your audience can be just as effective. Tools like Anchor can help you get started.

Choosing the Right Content Type for Your Audience

So how do you decide which content type is right for you? It all comes down to knowing your audience and understanding what will resonate with them. If your audience is busy professionals, maybe a podcast is the best way to reach them—they can listen while commuting or working out. If they're young and active on social media, short videos or Instagram posts might be the way to go.

You also need to think about what you're comfortable creating. If you hate being on camera, video might not be the best place to start. But if you love to write, blogging could be a perfect fit. The key is to start with something that feels natural so you can stay consistent.

Real-Life Examples of Content Success

Airbnb: Airbnb uses a mix of blog posts, videos, and user-generated content to showcase unique travel experiences. By highlighting their hosts and their guests' stories, they create content that feels personal and inspires others to travel.

Tasty (by BuzzFeed): Tasty uses short, fast-paced cooking videos that are incredibly shareable. They've tapped into the desire for quick, easy-to-follow recipes, and their videos reach millions of people. This kind of content works because it's visually engaging, easy to understand, and provides immediate value.

Moz: Moz, an SEO software company, has found success with in-depth blog posts and educational videos. Their content is targeted at marketers and SEO professionals who want to learn, and they provide content that is both informative and actionable.

Moving Forward

The takeaway here is that you don't need to do it all—you just need to do what works best for you and your audience. Think about who you're trying to reach, what kind of content they're most likely to engage with, and what you're comfortable creating. Start small, stay consistent, and remember that it's better to do one or two things really well than to spread yourself too thin trying to do it all.

In the next chapter, we're going to dive into how to set up a content marketing strategy from start to finish. It's all about planning ahead so you can be consistent and effective without feeling overwhelmed. Let's keep moving forward together.

CHAPTER # 4: SETTING UP A CONTENT MARKETING STRATEGY: PART 1

By now, you've got a solid understanding of what content marketing is and how powerful it can be for your small business. You've also seen how AI can make creating content a bit easier, and you've explored the different types of content and how to match them to your audience. Now, it's time to get into the nitty-gritty of setting up your content marketing strategy.

Creating a strategy is all about having a plan. Without a plan, you're just throwing content out there and hoping something sticks. A well-crafted strategy helps you focus your efforts, save time, and actually move toward your business goals. In this chapter, we'll take the first steps toward creating your content marketing strategy—starting with defining your goals, understanding your audience, and figuring out your unique voice.

Defining Your Goals and Objectives

The first step in setting up your content marketing strategy is to define your goals. Why are you doing this in the first place? What do you hope to achieve? Having a clear answer to these questions will help you create content that serves a purpose and drives results.

Your goals could be anything from increasing brand awareness to driving traffic to your website, generating leads, building an email list, or even boosting sales. The key is to make your goals specific and measurable. Instead of saying, "I want more customers," think about it in measurable terms like, "I want to generate 50 new leads this quarter." This way, you'll know whether or not your content strategy is working.

Here are a few common content marketing goals to consider:

Increase Brand Awareness: You want more people to know about your business. Content like blog posts, social media, and videos can help you reach a wider audience.

Engage Your Audience: You want to connect with your audience on a deeper level. Content like tutorials, podcasts, or Q&A sessions can help you engage and build relationships.

Drive Traffic to Your Website: You want to bring people to your website so they can learn more about your products or services. SEO-optimized blog posts and strategic social media shares can help.

Generate Leads: You want to collect contact information from potential customers. Content like e-books, webinars, or downloadable guides can help entice people to share their details.

Increase Sales: Ultimately, you want people to buy your product or service. Content like case studies, testimonials, and special offers can help persuade them.

Whatever your goals are, write them down. Be as specific as possible, and make sure they are aligned with your overall business objectives. Your content marketing strategy will revolve around these goals.

Identifying Your Target Audience

Once you've defined your goals, the next step is to understand who you're creating content for. This means getting crystal clear on your target audience—who are they, what do they care about, and how can your content help them?

Think about the people who are most likely to buy your products or services. What are their demographics? What challenges do they face, and what solutions are they looking for? The more you understand your audience, the better you'll be at creating content that resonates with them.

One way to get a deeper understanding of your audience is to create buyer personas. A buyer persona is a detailed description of your ideal customer. It goes beyond basic demographics and includes things like their interests, pain points, motivations, and even their preferred type of content.

For example, if you run a fitness studio, one of your personas might be "Working Mom Wendy," a 35-year-old mother of two who wants to stay fit but is short on time. Knowing Wendy's challenges (lack of time) and motivations (wants to stay healthy for her kids) can help you create content that speaks directly to her—like quick workout videos or blog posts on healthy meal prep for busy parents.

Finding Your Unique Voice

Now that you know what you want to achieve and who you're speaking to, it's time to figure out how you're going to communicate. This is where your "brand voice" comes in.

Your brand voice is the personality you bring to your content. It's how your business "sounds" when communicating with your audience. A consistent brand voice helps you stand out from the competition and makes your content feel more authentic. Are you casual and friendly? Professional and authoritative? Playful and humorous? The tone you use should reflect your brand and resonate with your target audience.

For example, if your audience is made up of small business owners who are juggling a million things, you might want to keep your tone conversational and down-to-earth. Avoid industry jargon, be relatable, and use real-life examples. On the other hand, if you're targeting CEOs or industry experts, your tone might be more formal and data-driven.

Take a moment to think about how you want your audience to feel when they interact with your content. Do you want them to feel inspired? Reassured? Excited? These feelings will help guide your brand voice. The key here is to be consistent—whether you're writing a blog post, filming a video, or posting on social media, your brand voice should feel familiar and true to who you are.

Putting It All Together

With your goals, audience, and brand voice defined, you're laying the foundation for a solid content marketing strategy. Remember, this process is all about getting clear on **why** you're creating content, **who** it's for, and **how** you're going to communicate. These foundational elements will guide everything you do moving forward.

In the next chapter, we'll dive into content planning—how to come up with content ideas, organize them into a content calendar, and make sure you're putting out content that aligns with your goals and resonates with your audience. But for now, take some time to think deeply about what you want to achieve, who you're speaking to, and how you're going to communicate. This is the foundation that will support your entire content marketing journey.

CHAPTER # 5: SETTING UP A CONTENT MARKETING STRATEGY - PART 2

Welcome back! By now, you've set the foundation for your content marketing strategy. You've figured out your goals and identified your audience. Now it's time to dive deeper into the nuts and bolts of planning. In this chapter, we'll be focusing on content themes, topics, and developing a content calendar. This is where the fun begins—where all those ideas start turning into action.

Content Themes and Topics

One of the biggest challenges for small business owners when it comes to content marketing is figuring out what to say. The key to making sure you're never at a loss for content is to have clear themes. **Content themes** are broad areas that you can talk about consistently, and they serve as the pillars of your content marketing strategy. Think of them as the main topics that are relevant to your business and interesting to your audience.

For example, if you're running a small home décor store, your content themes might include:

- ➤ **DIY Home Décor Projects:** Offering tips and ideas that inspire creativity.

- ➤ **Home Styling Inspiration:** How-to guides for different styles—boho, minimalist, farmhouse, etc.

- ➤ **Product Spotlights:** In-depth looks at the products you sell and how to use them effectively.

These themes will guide you in creating specific content that resonates with your audience while staying on brand. Once you have your themes, it's time to break them down into topics.

For the DIY Home Décor Projects theme, for example, some potential topics could be:

"How to Make Your Own Decorative Throw Pillows"

"Upcycling Old Furniture: A Beginner's Guide"

"3 Simple Ways to Create a Gallery Wall at Home"

Think of topics as the individual pieces that fit into the larger theme. Themes give you direction, while topics are the actual content you create.

Developing a Content Calendar

Once you have your themes and topics in place, the next step is to get organized. A content calendar is your roadmap for consistent content creation, and it's a lifesaver when it comes to staying on track. Without a calendar, it's easy to lose focus or run out of ideas, but with one, you'll always know what's coming up and what you need to prepare.

Your content calendar can be as simple or as detailed as you want it to be. Here's a basic approach to setting one up:

Choose Your Tools: You can use anything from a spreadsheet in Google Sheets to a more specialized tool like Trello or Asana. The key is to pick something that works for you and that you'll actually use.

Create Monthly or Weekly Plans: Start by planning on a monthly or weekly basis. It's good to have an overview of your content themes for the month and then break them down week by week. For example, the first week might focus on a DIY project, the second on styling inspiration, and so on.

CONTENT MARKETING STRATEGY

Add Deadlines and Responsibilities: If you have a team, include who's responsible for each piece of content and the deadlines. Even if it's just you, set deadlines for yourself. This helps keep you accountable and ensures your content stays consistent.

Include Distribution Plans: Remember, content creation is only half of the equation. You need to know where and how you're going to share each piece. Add notes on distribution—will it be shared on your blog, Instagram, in your newsletter, or all three?

A simple content calendar might look something like this:

Date	Content Theme	Topic	Format	Responsible	Distribution
Jan 5	DIY Home Décor Projects	How to Make Your Own Throw Pillows	Blog Post	Yourself	Blog, Instagram
Jan 12	Home Styling Inspiration	5 Ways to Style a Living Room	Instagram Carousel	Yourself	Instagram, Facebook
Jan 19	Product Spotlight	Spotlight on Handmade Rugs	Video	Team Member	Website, YouTube

Staying Flexible

One thing to remember about content calendars: stay flexible. Life happens, and sometimes you need to adjust your schedule. Maybe you get inspired to create a post that doesn't fit with what you originally planned, or maybe something unexpected comes up, and you need to push back a deadline. That's okay! The calendar is there to give you structure, but it shouldn't be so rigid that it stifles your creativity.

If you need to make changes, don't stress about it. Just update your calendar and move forward. The goal is to keep the process manageable and sustainable, not to overwhelm yourself.

Tools to Stay Organized

There are plenty of tools out there that can help you keep your content organized and on schedule. Here are a few favorites:

Trello: Trello is great for visual planning. You can create boards for each month, add cards for each piece of content, and easily move things around as needed.

Asana: If you like lists and tasks, Asana is an excellent choice. It allows you to assign tasks, set deadlines, and keep everything organized in one place.

Google Calendar: Sometimes, the simplest solution is the best one. You can create a content calendar directly in Google Calendar and add reminders to keep yourself on track.

Content Planning and Your Audience

Everything you plan should always come back to one thing: **your audience.** Think about what they want and need from you. When you're coming up with content themes and topics, put yourself in their shoes. What questions do they have? What problems are they trying to solve? What kind of content would make their lives a little easier or more enjoyable?

Your audience should be at the center of your content strategy. If you're always thinking about how you can provide value to them, you're going to create content that resonates, engages, and keeps them coming back for more.

Moving Forward

In the next chapter, we'll talk about creating the content itself—tips for keeping your content high-quality, balancing quantity and quality, and ensuring that your strategy remains sustainable over the long term. Now that you've got the planning piece in place, it's time to start bringing it all to life. Let's keep building this together, one step at a time.

CHAPTER # 6: SETTING UP A CONTENT MARKETING STRATEGY - PART 3

Creating a content marketing strategy is a journey that takes time, patience, and commitment. In this third part of setting up your content marketing strategy, we're diving into the best practices for content creation itself. This is where the magic happens—where your ideas start to take shape, and your content comes to life. Let's talk about balancing quality and quantity, staying consistent, and avoiding burnout while still making sure your content delivers value.

Content Creation Best Practices

Once you have a plan in place, the next step is to roll up your sleeves and start creating content. This might sound straightforward, but creating content that resonates with your audience, keeps them engaged, and helps build your brand is not always easy. Here are some best practices that will help you create content that stands out.

1. Quality Over Quantity

It's easy to get caught up in the idea that you need to create a constant flow of content. You've probably heard phrases like "content is king" or "the more content, the better." But here's the truth: quality always trumps quantity. It's better to create one really great piece of content that resonates with your audience than to churn out five mediocre ones that no one cares about.

Take the time to research, plan, and craft content that delivers real value. Whether it's a **blog post**, **video**, **podcast**, or **social media** update, your audience will notice the effort. High-quality content is more likely to be shared, engaged with, and remembered, and it helps build trust with your audience.

Pro Tip: Focus on providing actionable insights, helpful tips, or inspiring stories. Think about what your audience truly needs and how you can meet those needs with your content.

2. Create a Realistic Content Schedule

Consistency is key when it comes to content marketing. But consistency doesn't mean you need to post every single day. What matters is that you show up regularly, so your audience knows what to expect.

To do this, you need a realistic content schedule.

If you're just starting out, don't overwhelm yourself by trying to create content every day. Instead, start small—maybe one blog post a week, a video every other week, or three social media updates each week. The key is to find a schedule that works for you and stick to it.

3. Repurpose Your Content

Content creation doesn't always have to mean starting from scratch. One of the smartest ways to stay consistent without burning out is to repurpose your existing content. This means taking something you've already created and presenting it in a different format.

For example, if you wrote a blog post that performed well, consider turning it into a video, an infographic, or even a series of social media posts. Repurposing allows you to get more mileage out of your best content and ensures that you're reaching different segments of your audience.

Pro Tip: Use tools like Canva to easily create infographics or visual content from your existing material. This helps you reach a more visual audience without having to create entirely new content.

Balancing Quality and Quantity Without Burning Out

It's easy to fall into the trap of trying to do too much too quickly, especially when you're excited about your content marketing efforts. But burnout is a real risk, and it can happen to anyone. To avoid burnout, you need to strike a balance between quality and quantity.

1. Set Boundaries and Take Breaks

Running a small business means you're already wearing many hats. Content creation is just one of those responsibilities. It's important to set boundaries for yourself so you don't overdo it. If you're feeling overwhelmed, take a step back, reassess your schedule, and give yourself permission to take breaks.

Pro Tip: Block out specific time slots each week for content creation, and make sure you have designated days off. This way, you can focus on creating quality content without feeling like it's taking over your life.

2. Outsource When Needed

If you find that content creation is taking up too much of your time or you're struggling to stay consistent, consider outsourcing some of the work. Hiring a freelance writer, video editor, or social media manager can free up your time and allow you to focus on other aspects of your business.

Pro Tip: Platforms like Upwork or Fiverr can help you find talented freelancers to assist with content creation. You don't have to do it all by yourself.

3. Batch Create Content

One of the most effective ways to maintain consistency without burning out is to batch create content. This means setting aside time to create multiple pieces of content in one sitting. For example, you could spend one day writing three blog posts or filming several short videos.

Batching helps you stay ahead of schedule, reduces the pressure to constantly come up with new ideas, and makes the content creation process more efficient.

Pro Tip: Plan a monthly content batching day. Use this time to create and schedule as much content as possible so you're not constantly scrambling to come up with something new.

Content creation is where all your planning and strategizing finally come together, but it can be challenging to maintain quality, consistency, and avoid burnout. By focusing on quality over quantity, creating a realistic content schedule, repurposing existing content, and maintaining a consistent brand voice, you'll be well on your way to creating content that truly resonates with your audience.

Remember, content marketing is a marathon, not a sprint. Set boundaries, take breaks, and don't be afraid to ask for help when you need it. Consistency is important, but so is your well-being. Take it one step at a time, and soon enough, you'll have a content marketing strategy that works for you and helps your business grow.

In the next chapter, we'll dive into content distribution—how to get your content in front of the right audience so it actually makes an impact. Stay tuned!

CHAPTER # 7: SETTING UP A CONTENT MARKETING STRATEGY - PART 4

Content Distribution Strategies: Making Sure Your Content Get

By now, you've learned how to identify your audience, plan content themes, and develop an effective content calendar. You've also discovered best practices for content creation and how to maintain consistency. But even the best content will fall flat if no one sees it. That's why content distribution is such an important piece of the puzzle. If content creation is like cooking a great meal, distribution is getting that meal to the table—without this step, all that effort goes unnoticed.

Content distribution is about getting your content in front of the right people at the right time. It's the bridge that connects your message to your audience. You've put a lot of effort into creating content that's valuable and engaging, but without effective distribution, that content won't reach the people who need it most. Good content distribution requires a mix of understanding your audience's behaviors, using the right channels, and creating a cohesive strategy.

Since you're still reading this book—good! I haven't bored you to death—you now have most of the pieces to the puzzle. I mean, as far as "an introduction to content marketing" goes, we've covered some crucial ground so far. Getting our stuff out there so we can begin to engage, entertain, provoke thoughts—whatever you want your content to do—is the natural next topic to talk about.

In this chapter, we're going to explore the different ways you can distribute your content effectively, from social media to email marketing and beyond. The goal here is to help you maximize the reach and impact of your content, ensuring that it gets seen, engaged with, and ultimately drives the results you're looking for.

Leveraging Social Media

Social media is one of the most powerful tools for distributing content. However, not all platforms are created equal, and it's important to tailor your strategy to the unique strengths of each one. The truth is, my dear friend, you do not want to get into the habit of "platform-chasing." I know you know exactly what I mean by that. Even if you're not 100% sure, you kinda know, right? We've all done this—you try to set up an account for your company on every single platform you hear about. Facebook, LinkedIn, Twitter, Threads, Blurb, Bleep... at this point, I'm just making stuff up and you didn't even notice. That's my point.

As far as social media platforms go, we want to be, as the kids say, intentional. We want to 1) have a social media content distribution plan that is manageable and 2) relevant. We do not need to be everywhere all at once.

- Facebook: Great for building community, sharing articles, and engaging through comments and discussions. Facebook is ideal for content that tells a story or inspires conversation.

- Instagram: Perfect for highly visual content—images, short videos, Reels, and Stories. If your business has a strong visual component, Instagram should be a key part of your distribution strategy.

-LinkedIn: If you're in the B2B space or creating educational content, LinkedIn is a fantastic platform for reaching professionals. It's especially effective for sharing articles, insights, and thought leadership content.

- Twitter: Ideal for short, timely content. Use it for sharing news, quick updates, or links to your longer content pieces.

- **TikTok:** A rapidly growing platform that thrives on creativity and personality. If your audience is there, consider creating short, engaging videos that showcase your brand in a fun, relatable way.

The key with social media is to not spread yourself too thin. It's better to focus on one or two platforms and really engage with your audience than to try to be everywhere at once and have a minimal impact. Tailor your content to fit the platform and use tools like **buffer** or **Hootsuite** to schedule posts and stay organized.

The Power of Email Marketing

Email marketing is one of the most effective ways to distribute content. It allows you to communicate directly with your audience—people who have already shown interest in your business by subscribing to your list. The key to successful email content distribution is providing value, being consistent, and not overwhelming your subscribers.

-**Newsletters:** Send regular newsletters that include links to your latest blog posts, updates, or exclusive content. Keep them informative but concise, and make sure they're visually appealing.

-Segmented Campaigns: Segment your email list based on your subscribers' interests or behaviors, and send targeted content that's relevant to them. For example, if you run an online pet store, segment your list into cat owners and dog owners, and send content that speaks directly to their needs.

- Personalization: Use your subscribers' names, reference their past behavior (like previous purchases), and send content that feels personal. Personalized emails tend to perform better because they make your audience feel valued.

Tools like Benchmark Email or Beehiiv are great at infusing some Artificial intelligence and automation to help make your content distribution manageable.

Influencer Partnerships

Working with influencers is a great way to distribute content, especially if you want to expand your reach beyond your existing audience. Influencers have built trust with their followers, and a recommendation from them can carry a lot of weight.

You don't need to work with celebrity influencers—micro-influencers (those with smaller but highly engaged followings) can be incredibly effective, especially for small businesses. Reach out to influencers whose audiences align with yours, and see if they'd be interested in sharing your content, doing a product review, or collaborating on a piece of content.

Influencer partnerships can help you reach a wider audience, build credibility, and gain exposure that would be difficult to achieve on your own. Tools like upfluence or buzzsumo can help you find the right influencers for your niche.

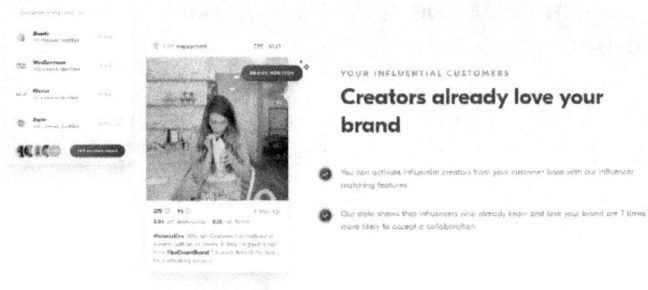

Paid Promotion

Sometimes, to get your content in front of the right people, you need to invest in paid promotion. Paid content distribution can help you reach a highly targeted audience and ensure that your content is being seen by the right people. Thanks to the power of technology and the various platforms out there with billions of users—ahem, Facebook!—you can, as a small business owner, set up a highly effective paid marketing strategy without going broke. What I'm trying to say is that you can have a small marketing budget and still make an impact.

Please do not listen to the folks out there who say that paying for ads is somehow not ideal. I'm not against organic growth—that's a good thing—but there's a reason why, as big as Walmart is, you still see their ads everywhere. Paying to get your stuff out there in front of the right people—whether it's content, products, services, etc.—should always be part of the plan. That being said, let's look at two of my favorite paid marketing channels.

Social Media Ads: Facebook, Instagram, LinkedIn, and Twitter all offer paid advertising options that allow you to promote your content to specific audiences. You can target based on demographics, interests, behaviors, and more.

Google Ads: If you have content that's educational or answers specific questions your audience might be searching for, consider using Google Ads to promote it. This can help drive traffic from people actively searching for topics related to your content.

On the other hand, you can also use tools like **Google Trends** to see relevant questions people are asking. Why? This way, you can create content that specifically answers the burning questions your audience has. Again, your content does not need to be directly related to your business or the services you offer—it only needs to be relevant to your audience.

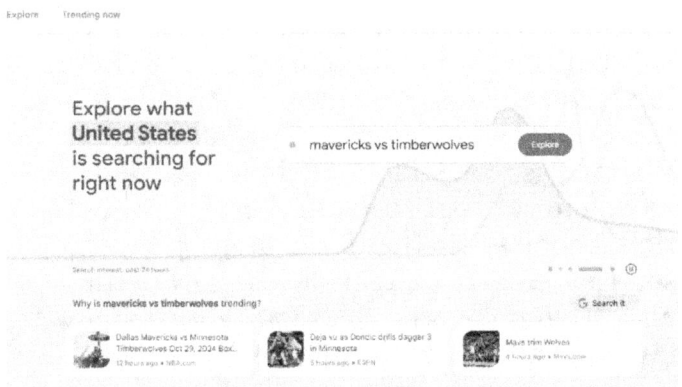

The key with paid promotion is to start small, measure your results, and adjust your strategy as needed. You don't need a huge budget—just a strategic approach that ensures your investment is paying off.

Content Syndication

Content syndication is the process of publishing your content on third-party sites to increase reach. This is particularly useful for getting more eyes on your articles, infographics, or videos. By partnering with industry websites, blogs, or other platforms, you can republish your content to reach new audiences.

Make sure to syndicate your content on sites

that align with your brand and where your target audience spends their time. Not only can syndication help you reach a larger audience, but it can also improve your SEO by driving more backlinks to your website.

We at Salesfully.com get dozens of requests a day from other small business owners asking us to publish and distribute their content to our thousands of users around the world. Over time, we have built a community of contributors and a handful of tools to help generate revenue, expand our brand, and help other small business owners grow their business and brand reach.

Once you become an expert at content marketing, perhaps you can also take a look at some of these ideas to help grow your business. One of our most popular programs in this area is our Content Partner program.

Repurposing Content

Content distribution doesn't always mean creating something new. Repurposing content is one of the smartest ways to extend the life of your work and reach different segments of your audience. For example, you could:

- ✓ Turn a blog post into a video.

- ✓ Create an infographic from key data points in an article.

- ✓ Break down a webinar into smaller social media clips.

- ✓ Take the best quotes from a podcast and turn them into shareable graphics.

The goal of repurposing is to adapt your content for different platforms and formats so that it reaches more people in the way they prefer to engage.

Content distribution is a crucial part of your content marketing strategy. Without it, all the hard work you put into creating content won't yield the results you're looking for. By leveraging social media, email marketing, influencer partnerships, paid promotion, content syndication, and repurposing, you can maximize the reach and impact of your content.

Remember, the goal is to meet your audience where they are. Choose the distribution methods that make the most sense for your audience and your business, and focus on quality over quantity. With a thoughtful content distribution strategy, you'll be able to amplify your message and connect with your audience in meaningful ways.

In the next chapter, we'll dive into how to measure the success of your content marketing strategy—because if you're putting in the work, you want to make sure it's paying off. Stay tuned!

CHAPTER # 8: MEASURING CONTENT MARKETING SUCCESS

Alright, so you've put in all the hard work—crafting great content, figuring out where to share it, and making sure it's getting in front of your target audience. But how do you know if it's actually working? How do you measure whether all the time and effort you've put into content marketing is paying off? In this chapter, we're going to dive into how you can effectively measure the success of your content marketing strategy. It's time to move beyond assumptions and start making data-driven decisions.

Why Measuring Success Matters

The truth is, if you're not measuring your content marketing efforts, you're essentially shooting in the dark. You need to know what's resonating with your audience and what's not. Without measuring, you won't be able to adjust your approach and optimize your results. Knowing what works helps you do more of it, and knowing what doesn't helps you avoid wasting valuable resources. Measurement is the key to evolving and improving your strategy over time. Do people comment on your content? What are they saying that you can use to improve your business or content? Do they save your content? Do they share it with others?

At Aromedy.com—one of our companies, a wellness platform—our main products are subscription boxes and health plan consulting. However, we share loads of content with our audience and also promote a lot of our articles, guides, and other content on social media. Once we started tracking our performance, we noticed that articles related to wellness, specifically those about how people access and use their health plans, got shared the most, and those always led to people calling us for help in setting up either a new plan or assistance with an existing one.

We get tons of questions via social media, email, text messages, etc., from people who need help navigating the complexities of health insurance. When people reach out to us, we always use that one-on-one time to help convert them into paying customers.

Key Metrics to Track

To determine the effectiveness of your content, it's crucial to track certain metrics. These metrics can provide insights into how your content is performing, who is engaging with it, and what type of impact it's having on your business. Here are some of the key metrics you should keep an eye on:

Traffic Metrics

- ➢ **Page Views:** This tells you how many times your content has been viewed. A high number of page views indicates strong interest in your topic.

- ➢ **Unique Visitors:** This metric reveals how many individual users are accessing your content, which can help you gauge your reach.

- ➢ **Traffic Sources:** Knowing where your audience is coming from—whether it's search engines, social media, or direct visits—can help you understand which channels are driving the most traffic.

Engagement Metrics

Time on Page: The longer someone stays on your page, the more engaged they are. It means they're finding your content valuable.

Bounce Rate: This measures the percentage of people who leave your site after viewing just one page. A high bounce rate might indicate that your content isn't grabbing attention or meeting expectations.

Social Shares and Comments: The more your content is shared or discussed, the more it's resonating with your audience.

Conversion Metrics

o **Lead Generation:** Is your content prompting users to sign up for your newsletter, download a guide, or fill out a contact form? This shows whether your content is effectively moving people through your sales funnel.

o **Sales and Revenue:** Ultimately, your content should drive sales. Are the people who engage with your content converting into paying customers?

Tools for Measuring Success

You don't have to measure all of this manually. There are several tools that can help you gather, analyze, and make sense of the data:

Google Analytics: This is a free tool that helps you track website traffic, page views, bounce rates, and more. It's a must-have for understanding how people are interacting with your content.

Google Search Console: This tool provides insight into how your content is performing in search results. It helps you see which keywords are bringing in traffic and any technical issues affecting your visibility.

Social Media Analytics: Most social media platforms offer analytics to help you understand how your posts are performing—metrics like reach, engagement, and follower growth.

HubSpot: If you're ready for a more advanced tool, HubSpot provides detailed insights into how your content is performing, from traffic and lead generation to conversions and sales.

Setting Goals and Benchmarks

To measure success effectively, it's important to establish clear goals and benchmarks. Here's how you can go about doing that:

Set SMART Goals: SMART stands for Specific, Measurable, Achievable, Relevant, and Time-bound. For instance, instead of setting a goal like "increase blog traffic," you could set a SMART goal like "increase blog traffic by 20% over the next three months." This goal is specific, measurable, and gives you a clear timeline.

Define KPIs: Your key performance indicators (KPIs) should align with your goals. If your goal is to increase brand awareness, your KPIs might include metrics like page views, social shares, and new visitors. If your goal is lead generation, KPIs might include email signups or contact form submissions.

Track Progress Regularly: Set up a schedule to review your metrics. This could be weekly, monthly, or quarterly, depending on your goals. Regular tracking allows you to make informed adjustments to your content strategy as needed.

The image above is an example of a content marketing dashboard. This type of dashboard allows you to visualize key metrics like page views, engagement rates, conversions, and more—all in one place. It's a great way to keep track of your progress at a glance and understand how your content is performing overall.

Analyzing and Adapting

Collecting data is only part of the process—you need to analyze it and make informed decisions based on your findings. Here's what to look for when analyzing your content's performance:

Identify Top-Performing Content: Look at the metrics to determine which pieces of content are getting the most engagement. Ask yourself why they're working—Is it the topic? The format? The distribution channel? Understanding what's working can help you create similar, high-performing content in the future.

Look for Opportunities to Improve: If you have content that isn't performing well, consider why that might be. Is the headline not compelling? Is the content too long or not providing enough value? Use your insights to make improvements.

Adapt and Test: Content marketing isn't a set-it-and-forget-it strategy. You should be constantly adapting and experimenting to see what works best for your audience. A/B testing different headlines, formats, or calls to action can provide valuable insights into what resonates most.

Measuring the success of your content marketing strategy is essential for making informed decisions that drive your business forward. By tracking key metrics, setting clear goals, and regularly analyzing your data, you'll be able to optimize your content strategy and ensure that it's delivering results. Remember, content marketing is a journey—stay committed, keep learning, and make adjustments along the way to achieve your goals.

In the next chapter, we'll explore the latest content marketing trends and how small businesses can stay ahead of the curve. Stay tuned!

CHAPTER # 9: EMERGING CONTENT MARKETING TRENDS

The world of content marketing is ever-evolving, and staying ahead of the curve is essential for small businesses looking to make an impact. In this chapter, we'll dive into some of the hottest emerging trends in content marketing that are shaping the industry today. Keeping an eye on these trends will help you stay relevant, engage your audience in fresh ways, and grow your brand.

Short-Form Video Content

One of the biggest trends in content marketing is the rise of short-form video content. Platforms like TikTok, Instagram Reels, and YouTube Shorts have redefined how we consume information. Short-form videos are perfect for capturing attention quickly and delivering a concise message that resonates with audiences. The beauty of this format is that it doesn't require an elaborate production setup—a smartphone and creativity are often enough.

If you haven't embraced short-form video yet, now is the time. Use these videos to show behind-the-scenes looks at your business, answer customer questions, or provide quick tips. The key is to be authentic and relatable, letting your audience get to know the person behind the brand.

Example: A local café could create 30-second clips showing how they prepare different types of coffee or showcasing customer reactions to trying a new pastry. These types of content keep customers engaged and build a deeper connection.

Interactive Content

Consumers no longer want to be passive viewers—they want to interact with content. Interactive content, such as polls, quizzes, and calculators, is gaining popularity because it keeps people engaged longer and provides value that feels personalized.

Consider adding interactive elements to your content strategy to boost engagement. Quizzes like "What Type of Workout Fits You Best?" or interactive infographics that allow users to explore data can be powerful tools to capture and maintain attention.

Example: A fitness studio could use a simple quiz to help website visitors identify which of their classes would be the best fit based on their fitness goals and experience level. This type of content provides value and encourages participation, increasing the likelihood of conversion.

Personalized Content

Personalization is becoming increasingly important, especially as customers expect tailored experiences. Using data to create personalized content allows you to cater specifically to the needs and preferences of your audience, which builds trust and encourages loyalty.

Email marketing, for example, can be greatly enhanced with personalization. Instead of sending out a one-size-fits-all newsletter, segment your audience and craft specific messages for each group. Personalized content can also apply to blog posts, product recommendations, or even tailored landing pages.

Example: An online clothing retailer could send targeted emails to customers based on their browsing history, such as featuring summer dresses for those who have been looking at warm-weather attire. Personalized product recommendations can lead to increased conversions and repeat business.

Audio Content and Voice Search Optimization

Podcasts and audio content are on the rise. People are busier than ever, and audio content allows them to multitask—whether they're commuting, working out, or cooking dinner. If you haven't considered incorporating audio content into your strategy, it's worth exploring. You could start a podcast related to your industry, share interviews with industry experts, or even provide short audio clips on your blog posts.

In addition to audio content, it's also important to optimize for voice search. More and more people are using smart speakers like Alexa or Google Home to find information. Voice searches tend to be longer and more conversational, so optimizing your content to answer common questions in a natural way will help you get found.

User-Generated Content (UGC)

User-generated content is another major trend in content marketing. UGC refers to content created by your customers—photos, videos, reviews, or testimonials. It's authentic, and audiences love it because it showcases real people enjoying your products or services.

Encouraging your customers to share their experiences not only gives you more content to use but also builds social proof. People are more likely to trust other customers than they are to trust a brand directly, so showcasing UGC can make a big impact.

Example: A skincare brand could encourage its customers to share their before-and-after photos using a branded hashtag. By resharing these photos on their social media channels, the brand gains credibility and builds a community of loyal customers.

Collaborations and Influencer Partnerships

Collaborations and influencer partnerships are also powerful strategies in today's content landscape. Partnering with others allows you to leverage their audience while providing value to your own. Whether you collaborate with a local business or work with a micro-influencer in your niche, these partnerships can lead to great results.

Micro-influencers, who have smaller but highly engaged audiences, are particularly effective for small businesses. They provide authenticity and relatability that large influencers often lack. By working with someone who shares your brand values, you can create impactful content that feels genuine and reaches new potential customers.

CONTENT MARKETING STRATEGY

The world of content marketing is changing rapidly, and small businesses that stay ahead of the trends will have the best chance of success. Whether it's diving into short-form video, adding personalization, embracing user-generated content, or collaborating with others, there are plenty of exciting ways to keep your content fresh and engaging.

The key is to experiment, be willing to try new things, and see what works best for your audience. Content marketing is not a one-size-fits-all solution, and the more you can adapt to emerging trends, the more effective your strategy will be.

In the next chapter, we'll look at how small businesses can leverage collaboration to create and distribute content effectively, taking your content strategy even further.

CHAPTER # 10: COLLABORATIVE CONTENT MARKETING

Amplify Your Reach by Partnering with Others

As we wrap things up, I want to highlight a powerful content marketing strategy that is often underutilized—collaborative content marketing. You see, we've talked a lot about creating and distributing content on your own, but there's a whole other side to content marketing that involves working together. Collaboration can be one of the most effective ways for small businesses to amplify their reach, share resources, and create more impactful content. Let's talk a bit about how you can leverage collaborative content marketing to take your strategy to the next level.

The Power of Collaboration

Content marketing can be challenging, especially when you're working solo or with a small team. The idea of coming up with fresh content consistently, managing distribution channels, and keeping your audience engaged can feel overwhelming. This is where collaboration comes in—it allows you to share the workload, cross-promote each other's content, and ultimately reach a larger audience than you could on your own.

Think of collaboration as a way to tap into someone else's audience, while they do the same with yours. It's a win-win that not only expands your reach but also brings new voices and ideas into your content, making it more engaging for your audience.

Types of Collaborative Content Marketing

There are many different ways to collaborate on content. Here are some of the most effective methods:

Guest Blogging: One of the simplest ways to collaborate is by guest blogging. Find businesses that have a similar audience but aren't direct competitors, and offer to write a blog post for their site. In return, they could write one for yours. This helps introduce your brand to their audience and vice versa.

Joint Social Media Campaigns: Running a social media campaign together can be a great way to generate buzz. For example, if you're a fitness coach and you team up with a nutritionist, you could run a campaign around healthy living, with each of you sharing content that complements the other's expertise.

Co-Hosted Webinars or Workshops: This is particularly effective if you want to provide in-depth value. Let's say you're a financial consultant—partner with a business coach to host a webinar on "Managing Finances and Growing Your Business." This way, you provide comprehensive value, and both of your audiences benefit.

Podcast Guest Appearances: If you or a collaborator have a podcast, invite each other as guests. This not only brings fresh insights to your audience but also exposes both of you to new listeners.

Finding the Right Partners

Finding the right partner is crucial for successful collaboration. Here are some things to consider when looking for a collaborator:

Shared Audience: Look for businesses that share a similar audience but offer different products or services. This means you're not in direct competition, but you're still talking to the same group of people.

Aligned Values: It's important to find a partner whose values align with yours. This ensures that the collaboration feels authentic and that the message resonates well with both audiences.

Mutual Benefit: Successful collaborations are built on mutual benefit. Make sure both parties are getting something out of the partnership, whether it's exposure, leads, or content.

Real-Life Examples of Successful Collaborations

Starbucks & Spotify: Starbucks partnered with Spotify to create an engaging experience for their customers. Starbucks' loyalty members could influence in-store playlists, providing a unique connection between music and coffee culture. This collaboration benefited both brands by connecting music lovers with the Starbucks environment.

GoPro & Red Bull: GoPro and Red Bull teamed up for content around extreme sports. Red Bull's brand is all about high-energy, action-packed experiences, and GoPro's cameras capture those moments. By collaborating, they created visually stunning content that appealed to both audiences.

How to Get Started

Ready to get started with collaborative content marketing? Here are some simple steps to follow:

Identify Potential Partners: Think about

businesses that align well with yours. Make a list of brands that share your audience and values.

Reach Out: Don't be afraid to reach out. Send a friendly email or message explaining why you think a collaboration could benefit both of you.

Brainstorm Ideas: Once you have a partner on board, start brainstorming ideas for content. Think about what each of you does best and how you can combine those strengths.

Plan and Execute: Put together a simple plan, set deadlines, and make it happen! Whether it's a joint social media campaign or a co-hosted webinar, make sure you're both on the same page about expectations.

Collaboration Best Practices

Communication is Key: Make sure you communicate clearly with your collaborator. Set expectations upfront and stay in touch throughout the process.

Track Performance: Just like with your own content, track the performance of your collaborative content. Did it reach more people than your regular posts? Did it drive more engagement? Use these insights for future collaborations.

Celebrate Success: Once your collaboration is complete, celebrate your success together. Share the results with your audience and thank your partner publicly. This not only shows appreciation but also encourages future collaborations.

Collaborative content marketing is one of the most effective ways for small businesses to amplify their reach, share resources, and create more impactful content. Whether you're co-writing a blog, hosting a joint webinar, or partnering for a social media campaign, collaboration can help you achieve far more than you could alone.

Remember, content marketing doesn't have to be a solo endeavor. By working together, we can create richer, more engaging content and reach audiences that might have otherwise been out of reach. It's all about community, shared growth, and helping each other succeed.

With this final chapter, we close our journey into content marketing for small business owners. I hope you now feel equipped to take on content marketing with a clear plan and a sense of confidence. Remember, stay consistent, be creative, and don't be afraid to ask for help or collaborate. Content marketing is all about building relationships, and what better way to do that than by working together?

Let's take this journey one step further,

together. Here's to your success in content marketing and beyond!

Resources

Throughout this book, we've covered a lot of ground in content marketing, and I've mentioned various tools and resources to help you along the way. Below, you'll find a list of all the resources referenced, with links to make it easy for you to explore them.

Content Creation Tools

Canva: An easy-to-use design tool for creating social media graphics, infographics, and other visuals.
https://www.canva.com/

Grammarly: A writing assistant that helps catch grammar mistakes and improve readability.
Grammarly

InShot: A video editing app perfect for creating short-form content for social media.
InShot

CapCut: Another simple and effective video editor for short content.
CapCut

Content Distribution Tools

Buffer: A tool to schedule social media posts in advance.
Buffer

Hootsuite: Another social media management platform to help you plan and schedule posts.
Hootsuite

Mailchimp: An email marketing service that helps you manage campaigns and segment your audience.
Mailchimp

ActiveCampaign: A marketing automation tool that allows you to personalize your email content.
ActiveCampaign

Analytics and Measurement Tools

Google Analytics: Essential for tracking website traffic, engagement, and conversions.
Google Analytics

Google Search Console: Helps you track how your content is performing in search results.
Google Search Console

HubSpot: A powerful tool for tracking all aspects of content marketing, from traffic to customer engagement.
HubSpot

CONTENT MARKETING STRATEGY

BuzzSumo: A platform for finding influencers and tracking trending content in your niche.
BuzzSumo

Interactive Content Tools

Typeform: A tool to create interactive quizzes, surveys, and forms.
Typeform

Outgrow: A platform to create calculators, quizzes, and other interactive content.
Outgrow

Collaboration and Influencer Marketing Tools

Upfluence: A tool to find influencers for potential collaboration.
Upfluence

Zoom: A popular platform for hosting webinars and virtual workshops.
Zoom

Webex: Another great tool for virtual events and meetings.
Webex

Podcasting Tools

Anchor: A free tool for creating and distributing podcasts.
Anchor

Google Notebook LM: NotebookLM, a tool that helps users understand complex information by summarizing sources and providing relevant quotes, now offers an "Audio Overview" feature.
Notebook LM

All NotebookLM

Queries   Sources

Think Smarter,
Not Harder

The ultimate tool for understanding the information that matters most to you, built with Gemini 1.5

Try NotebookLM

Your Personalized AI Research Assistant

Rss.com: A platform that allows you to host and distribute your podcast to all the major podcasting platforms out there.
Rss.com

SEO and Keyword Research Tools

Ahrefs: A platform for keyword research and backlink analysis.
Ahrefs

CONTENT MARKETING STRATEGY

Google Keyword Planner: Helps you identify relevant keywords for your content.
Google Keyword Planner

Google Trends: Helps you see what topics are trending in your industry.
Google Trends

These resources can help you create, distribute, analyze, and improve your content marketing efforts. Take the time to explore each tool and see how it can fit into your strategy.

Remember, the right tools can make a huge difference in your content marketing journey.

CONTENT MARKETING STRATEGY

CONTENT MARKETING STRATEGY

DISCLAIMERS:

The following disclaimer is intended to provide important information regarding the author, Frank Dappah, and the publisher, OSTRICH Publishers. Please read this disclaimer carefully before engaging with any content published by or associated with Frank Dappah and OSTRICH Publishers.

FRANK DAPPAH:

Frank Dappah is the author of the book discussed in this text. While efforts have been made to provide accurate and up-to-date information, the author cannot guarantee the completeness, accuracy, or reliability of the content presented. The views expressed in the book are solely those of the author and do not necessarily reflect the views of any individuals, organizations, or institutions mentioned within the text.

Frank Dappah is an experienced entrepreneur and sales professional. However, it is important to recognize that individual experiences and outcomes may vary. The examples and anecdotes shared by the author are intended for illustrative purposes only and should not be construed as guarantees of success or financial results.

The information provided in this book is not intended to serve as professional business or financial advice. Readers are advised to consult with qualified professionals or seek independent advice before making any business or financial decisions based on the content of this book.

OSTRICH PUBLISHERS:

OSTRICH Publishers is the publishing company responsible for publishing the book written by Frank Dappah. While the publisher endeavors to ensure the accuracy and quality of the published material, OSTRICH Publishers cannot be held responsible for any errors, omissions, or discrepancies that may be present within the book.

OSTRICH Publishers is not liable for any direct, indirect, incidental, consequential, or other damages arising out of or in connection with the book, its content, or any reliance placed upon it. The publisher does not endorse any specific products, services, or organizations mentioned in the book unless explicitly stated.

GENERAL INFORMATION:

The content of this book is provided for informational purposes only. It is not intended to substitute professional advice or guidance. Readers should exercise their own judgment and discretion when applying the concepts, strategies, or suggestions presented in the book.

All trademarks, registered trademarks, or logos mentioned in the book are the property of their respective owners. The inclusion of any external links or references within the book does not imply endorsement or approval by the author or publisher.

The author and publisher disclaim any liability for the accuracy, reliability, or availability of information contained within the book. They are not responsible for any loss or damage that may arise from the use of the book or its content.

In conclusion, readers are advised to use their discretion, seek professional advice, and conduct their own research before making any business, financial, or personal decisions. The author and publisher shall not be held responsible for any consequences, direct or indirect, arising from the use or interpretation of the information provided in the book.

By accessing and engaging with the content published by Frank Dappah and OSTRICH Publishers, you acknowledge and accept the terms of this disclaimer.

CONTENT MARKETING STRATEGY

CONTENT MARKETING STRATEGY

Thank you!

Thank you so much for being a part of my literary journey and allowing me to share my thoughts and insights with you.

I strive to create books that provide value and contribute to the knowledge and understanding of various topics. Your feedback is incredibly valuable to me and plays a vital role in shaping my writing style and the subjects I explore.

At OSTRICH, we greatly appreciate the feedback we receive from readers like you. It helps us improve and deliver content that is engaging and meaningful.

We are committed to our mission of creating captivating and informative material, and your input is instrumental in achieving that goal.

I invite you to visit our website at www.ostrichpress.com or check out our books on platforms like Amazon, Kobo, and Google Play. Your thoughts and opinions matter to us, and we would love to hear your feedback on this book or any others you may have read.

Once again, thank you for your support and for being a part of this journey. Your engagement and feedback are truly appreciated.

Warm regards,
Frank Dappah

ABOUT THE AUTHOR

Frank is a charismatic and visionary entrepreneur, accomplished author, and seasoned investor. With a passion for business and a wealth of experience, Frank has written extensively on topics ranging from marketing and social media to entrepreneurship and beyond. His insightful books have garnered praise for their practical advice and actionable strategies.

Living in the vibrant city of Charlotte, North Carolina, Frank thrives on the dynamic energy of the business world. Alongside his partner and wife, Bernice, he has built successful ventures and continues to explore new opportunities in the ever-evolving landscape of entrepreneurship.

Frank's unique perspective and expertise make him a sought-after speaker and advisor, empowering aspiring entrepreneurs to unlock their full potential. With his engaging writing style and knack for simplifying complex concepts, Frank has helped countless readers navigate the challenges and seize the opportunities that come with starting and growing their own businesses.

When he's not immersed in his entrepreneurial endeavors, Frank enjoys spending quality time with his family, exploring the outdoors, and indulging his love for movies, books, and astronomy. His curiosity knows no bounds, and he is always eager to delve into new subjects and expand his knowledge.

Connect with Frank on social media and join him on this exciting journey of innovation, growth, and success.

MY OTHER BOOKS

TURN OFF AND THEN ON AGAIN: REBOOTING YOUR PSYCHOLOGICAL OPERATING SYSTEM

In a world filled with constant noise and distractions, it's easy to lose sight of who we truly are and what we truly want. discovery and personal growth? If so, "Turn Off and Then On Again: Rebooting Your Psychological Operating System" is the guidebook you've been waiting for.

**GODSPLAINING EVERYTHING:
EXPLAINING GOD-SIZED PARADOXES
THROUGH FAITH AND REASON!**
*Experience a profound exploration of
spirituality, belief systems, and the human quest
for understanding in "Godsplaining
Everything." Delve into the multifaceted aspects
of religion, faith, skepticism, and the
complexities that shape our diverse world.*

OUR BIG, BEAUTIFULLY STRANGE UNIVERSE: A NON-ASTRONOMER'S TAKE ON THE MARVELS OF COSMOLOGY

Are you ready for an adventure into the mind-bending wonders of the cosmos? Join Frank Dappah, an entrepreneur with an insatiable passion for astronomy and physics, as he takes you on an exhilarating journey through the realms of our vast and enigmatic universe.

CONTENT MARKETING STRATEGY

CONTENT MARKETING STRATEGY

OSTRICH PUBLISHERS: WHO WE ARE!

Welcome to Ostrich Publishers, an innovative and inclusive publishing and distribution platform dedicated to empowering talented independent authors and creatives worldwide. At Ostrich, our mission is to provide a robust medium through which these individuals can share their works with the rest of the world.

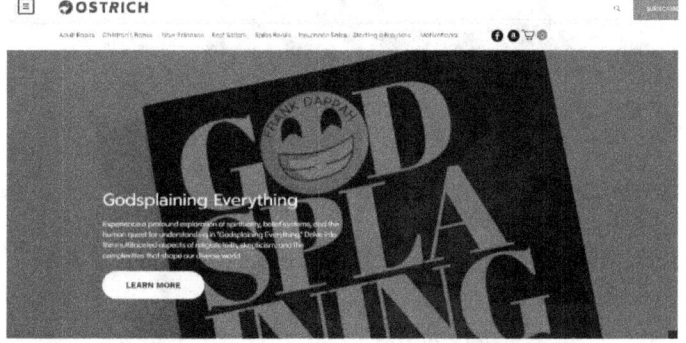

https://www.ostrichpress.com/about

We believe that every author, regardless of their background, deserves the opportunity to have their voice heard and their stories told. To accomplish this, we work closely with authors throughout the entire publishing journey. From the initial brainstorming stage to the final distribution and marketing process, we are committed to supporting authors every step of the way.

Our strength lies in our comprehensive distribution infrastructure, which enables us to reach global audiences and ensure that authors receive the recognition they deserve. By leveraging our platform, authors who might have otherwise gone unnoticed can now showcase their talents and connect with readers worldwide.

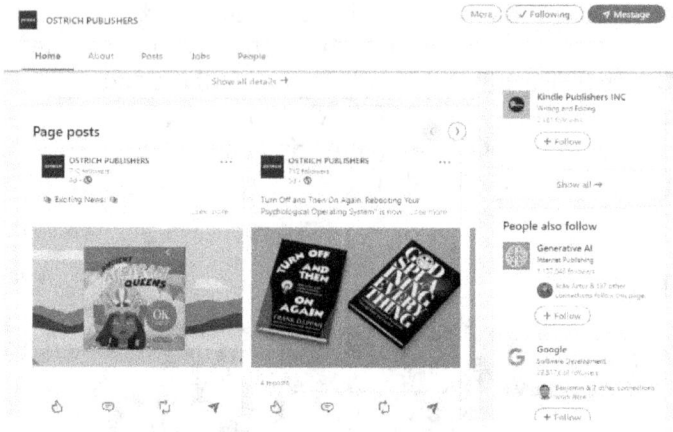

https://bit.ly/44kA6w5

At Ostrich, we prioritize collaboration, creativity, and inclusivity. We are dedicated to fostering an environment where authors can thrive, providing them with the tools, resources, and guidance they need to bring their works to life. By embracing technology and innovation, we are building an all-inclusive publishing and distribution platform that opens doors for authors from diverse backgrounds.

Join us on this exciting journey as we revolutionize the publishing industry and amplify the voices of independent authors and creatives. Together, we can bring captivating stories, compelling ideas, and inspiring works to readers around the globe.

CONTENT MARKETING STRATEGY

CONTENT MARKETING STRATEGY

OSTRICH®

CONTENT MARKETING STRATEGY

CONTENT MARKETING STRATEGY

So You're Sorta Thinking About Starting an awesomely effective

Content Marketing Strategy?

A Beginner's Guide to Content Marketing for Small Business Owners: Simple Steps to Grow Your Brand and Engage Your Audience

frank dappah

CONTENT MARKETING STRATEGY

CONTENT MARKETING STRATEGY

CONTENT MARKETING STRATEGY

OSTRICH PUBLISHERS

Published by Ostrich Publishing Group

Charlotte, North Carolina 28212, U.S.A

First published in the United States of America by Ostrich Publishing Group, an Independent Book publisher.

9798851605864

Copyright © 2022 Ostrich Publishers

www.ostrichpress.com

All rights reserved.

ISBN: 9798851605864

Except in the United States of America, this book is sold subject to the conditions that is shall not, by way of trade or otherwise, be lent, re-sold, hired out, or otherwise circulated without the publisher's prior consent in any form of binding or cover other than in which is it published and without a similar condition including this condition being imposed on the subsequent purchaser.

CONTENT MARKETING STRATEGY

CONTENT MARKETING STRATEGY

So You're Sorta Thinking About Starting an awesomely effective

Content Marketing Strategy?

⌐A Beginner's Guide to Content Marketing for Small Business Owners: Simple Steps to Grow Your Brand and Engage Your Audience ⌐

frank dappah

CONTENT MARKETING STRATEGY

CONTENT MARKETING STRATEGY

OSTRICH®

CONTENT MARKETING STRATEGY

CONTENT MARKETING STRATEGY

Publisher's Disclaimer:

The information contained in this publication is for general informational purposes only. While we have made every effort to provide accurate and up-to-date information, we make no representations or warranties of any kind, express or implied, about the completeness, accuracy, reliability, suitability, or availability with respect to the content contained herein. Any reliance you place on such information is therefore strictly at your own risk.

Content Accuracy:

The content in this publication is based on the knowledge and information available at the time of writing. However, developments in the field may occur after publication, and the publisher cannot guarantee that the information provided will always be complete, accurate, or up-to-date. Readers are advised to consult additional sources and seek professional advice where necessary.

Editorial Responsibility:

The views and opinions expressed by the authors, contributors, and editors of this publication are their own and do not necessarily reflect the views of Ostrich Publishers. The publisher disclaims any liability or responsibility for any errors, omissions, or inaccuracies that may be present in the content.

Legal Compliance:

While every effort has been made to ensure compliance with all applicable laws and regulations, the publisher cannot be held responsible for any legal implications or consequences arising from the use or misuse of the information in this publication. Readers are advised to familiarize themselves with the relevant laws and seek legal counsel if necessary.

Third-Party Content:

This publication may include content from third-party sources, including but not limited to quotes, references, or excerpts. Ostrich Publishers does not endorse or guarantee the accuracy, reliability, or suitability of any third-party content referenced in this publication. Any reliance on such content is at the reader's own discretion and risk.

External Links:

This publication may contain links to external websites or resources. Ostrich Publishers has no control over the nature, content, and availability of those sites or resources. The inclusion of any links does not necessarily imply a recommendation or endorsement by the publisher. Ostrich Publishers shall not be held liable for any damages or losses arising from the use of such external links.

CONTENT MARKETING STRATEGY

Copyright:

All rights reserved. No part of this publication may be reproduced, distributed, or transmitted in any form or by any means, including photocopying, recording, or other electronic or mechanical methods, without the prior written permission of the publisher, except in the case of brief quotations embodied in critical reviews and certain other noncommercial uses permitted by copyright law.

Contact Information:

For inquiries regarding this publication, please contact:

Ostrich Publishers
Charlotte, NC
U.S.A
Email: admin@ostrichpress.com
Website: www.ostrichpress.com

Disclaimer Updates:

Ostrich Publishers reserves the right to amend or update this disclaimer at any time without prior notice. It is the responsibility of the readers to regularly review this disclaimer for any changes.

Last Updated:
May 202

CONTENT MARKETING STRATEGY

OSTRICH®

CONTENT MARKETING STRATEGY

CONTENT MARKETING STRATEGY

OSTRICH®

CONTENT MARKETING STRATEGY

www.ingramcontent.com/pod-product-compliance
Lightning Source LLC
Chambersburg PA
CBHW052323220526
45472CB00001B/241